*The Mackinac Bridge, spanning the Straits of Mackinac and con-
necting the Upper and Lower Peninsulas of Michigan, stands as one
of man's greatest engineering and construction achievements. Bridging
five miles of open water which was formerly served only by ferries, the
crossing is made in minutes, where previously delays of 36 hours and
longer could be encountered. Designed by Dr. D. B. Steinman, the bridge
has been engineered to withstand many times the recorded stresses of ice
pressure, wind velocity, gravity, etc. Construction began in 1954 and the
bridge was opened to traffic on November 1, 1957.*

Straits
of Mackinac

A vital link in the world's greatest inland waterway, the St. Lawrence Seaway, the Straits provide the only link between Lake Huron and Lake Michigan. The Straits also separate the Upper and Lower Peninsulas of the State of Michigan and is the focal point of land and water access to the upper Great Lakes region.

Mackinaw City and St. Ignace, at either end of the Mackinac Bridge, are your host cities at the Straits. Museums depicting the rich history of the area, pageantry portraying historical events conducted by local citizens, excellent motels and hotels, fine restaurants serving a variety of cuisine, camping facilities, rest areas and parks, are provided for your convenience and comfort while guests of these hospitable cities.

Old Mackinac Point Lighthouse, built in 1892, served the Straits until the Mackinac Bridge was completed in 1957. It is located in Fort Michilimackinac State Park.

Fort Michilimackinac

*T*he fort was built by the French in 1714-15 and has been restored to capture the atmosphere of two centuries ago.

Under treaty between the two powers, the French soldiers and their families left the fort and the English took control. Unhappy under the English control, the Indians, led by Chief Pontiac, plotted to overthrow the fort.

Using the game of Bagataway, they drew the soldiers out of the fort to watch the game. Indian squaws, standing near the gates, concealed knives and tomahawks under their blankets. At a precise moment, the Indians armed themselves and attacked the British soldiers, storming inside the fort through the open gates. When the fateful day in 1763 ended, the British were driven from the fort with 21 killed. Only four Englishmen lived to tell the story. They escaped to Mackinac Island and went into hiding for several days.

In 1780-81, development of Mackinac Island began with the building of a new fort, Fort Mackinac, high above the natural harbor overlooking the Straits. The fur trading post then moved from Fort Michilimackinac to Mackinac Island, thus ending one era and beginning another.

On Memorial Day weekend, citizens of Mackinaw City annually present a colorful pageant, depicting the historic events at this frontier outpost.

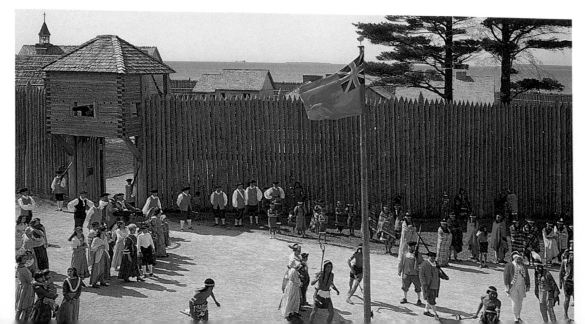

A colonial woman plays the fiddle in preparation of the French wedding re-enactment performed twice daily.

British red-coated soldiers at Colonial Michilimackinac fire their muskets several times daily in the reconstructed fort and fur-trading village.

Photo: Mackinac State Historic Park

Photo: Mackinac State Historic Park

The King's Garden

*F*ort Michilimackinac is restored and history comes alive as visitors are given guided tours and demonstrations of pioneer life at Mackinac.

A military drummer stands proudly in front of the British Union Jack at Colonial Michilimackinac in Mackinaw City.

Photo: Mackinac State Historic Park

4

Old Mill Creek

*A*s more people came to the Straits region, the need for building materials increased.

Old Mill Creek is a state park located between Mackinaw City and Cheboygan. A replica sawmill stands on the original site. Operated by water power, it is a working sawmill. Guides demonstrate and explain the logging operations and show how timber was made into finished lumber. Much of the lumber from this mill was used on Mackinac Island.

Old Mill Creek is a most interesting attraction in a very picturesque setting. Anyone visiting the Straits should take time to visit and enjoy it.

Vessels and Ships

*T*HE WELCOME. *This sailing vessel was built at Fort Michilimackinac at Mackinaw City. It is a replica of the original Welcome which was one of the first vessels to sail in the Straits area.*

*C*HIEF WAWATAM. *Built in 1911, the railroad car ferry carried freight cars across the Straits between Mackinaw City and St. Ignace for 73 years. With six hand fired coal burning boilers, it could carry from 16 to 22 railroad cars.*

*V*ACATIONLAND. This ice-breaking automobile ferry was constructed specifically for the Straits of Mackinac. It was one of the most powerful ships on the Great Lakes with four diesel engines generating 10,000 horsepower. The ship could move in either direction with equal ability due to its twin props and pilothouses built on both ends. The 360 foot ship began operation in 1952 and could hold 150 cars and 650 passengers.

*T*HE STRAITS OF MACKINAC. Built in 1928, the ship became the smallest of the automobile ferry fleet between Mackinaw City and St. Ignace. After the building of the Mackinac Bridge it was used for several years to carry passengers between Mackinac Island and Mackinaw City. It had a capacity of 1000 passengers.

*C*ITY OF MUNISING. Formerly a railroad ship, it was purchased, reconditioned and began service in 1938 as an automobile ferry across the Straits. In 1947 a new bow and forward loading ramps were built bringing the length to 339 feet with a capacity of 120 cars.

St. Ignace

*T*he geography of St. Ignace made it the most suitable place for the first settlement in this region. The natural sheltered harbor provided access to not only the Straits area but the entire Great Lake frontier.

Visitors and residents alike walk the same ground used by many Indians and famous Frenchmen, such as Marquette, Cadillac, Tonty, Allouez, Joliet and DuLhut. Father Marquette founded a mission at St. Ignace in 1671, making it the second oldest settlement in Michigan. Sault Ste. Marie, 60 miles north, was the first settlement in 1668. Marquette named his mission St. Ignace de Missilmakinak, to honor St. Ignatious Loyola, founder of the Jesuit order. Father Marquette, famous missionary and explorer throughout the Upper Peninsula, is buried at St. Ignace. His body was returned here in 1677 after his death in 1675 at Ludington.

GRAVE OF FATHER MARQUETTE
(Translation of Latin Text on Monument)
IN MEMORIAM
Erected by the citizens of St. Ignace in 1882, this monument marks the grave of Rev. Father James Marquette, S.J., who died on the eighteenth day of May, 1675, at the age of thirty eight and was buried here, in 1677.
R. I. P.

*T*his ship was originally built by the US Lighthouse Service. Now a museum, the Maple is the oldest USCG Cutter to have served on the Great Lakes.

USCG Cutter Maple

Founded 1671

*F*rom its humble beginnings as a mission and fur trading center, St. Ignace has become a hospitality center for visitors crossing the Mackinac Bridge to the Upper Peninsula, as well as for many going by ferry boat to Mackinac Island.

It was an important shipping port during the lumbering era in Michigan. Today it is a major crossroads both by land and water. Interstate I-75 is the primary North-South route and U.S. 2 the East-West. From the high bluffs, one can watch ships and super ore carriers pass through the Straits between Lake Michigan and Lake Huron.

There are many stores and gift shops, motels, restaurants and attractions to make a visit enjoyable. Many visitors make St. Ignace their headquarters for day trips to other Upper Peninsula attractions such as the Soo Locks, Tahquamenon Falls and the Pictured Rocks.

Many of the present day St. Ignace residents are descendents of the early day French and Indian settlers.

*M*arquette Mission Park and Museum of Ojibwa Culture, a National Historic landmark in downtown St. Ignace, interprets the rich archaeology and history of a 17th century Huron Indian village, a French Jesuit Mission, and local Ojibwa Indian Culture. Open daily, Memorial Day weekend to Mid-October, the museum store features certified Native American art and crafts.

*C*astle Rock, often referred to as "Pontiac's Lookout," is located three miles north of St. Ignace. This ancient lookout of the Ojibwa rises from the surrounding lowlands like a castle of the middle ages. Reaching a height of 195.8 feet above water level and 183 feet above road level the view from its summit is inspiring.

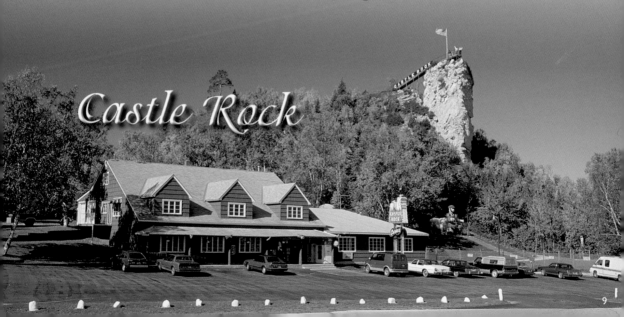

Castle Rock

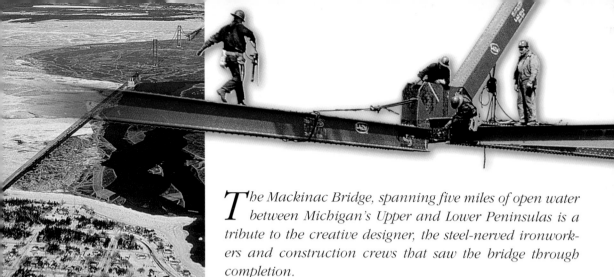

*T*he Mackinac Bridge, spanning five miles of open water between Michigan's Upper and Lower Peninsulas is a tribute to the creative designer, the steel-nerved ironworkers and construction crews that saw the bridge through completion.

Building the impossible bridge

*C*onstruction of the bridge got underway and ground-breaking ceremonies were held in the spring of 1954. Throughout 1954 a fleet of tugs and barges worked completing the water-based piers. During 1955 the above-water portions of the piers and the steel towers took shape. In 1956 the catwalks were strung and the work of stringing the cables progressed around the clock. The structure began to take on the appearance of a bridge. Early in 1957 the superstructure construction began outward from each tower. By mid-summer the span was joined in the center. Next to come was the roadway grid construction and, ready for traffic, the bridge was opened November 1, 1957.

The Bridge at Mackinac

By D. B. Steinman

In the land of Hiawatha,
  Where the white man gazed with awe
At a paradise divided
  By the Straits of Mackinac-

Men are dredging, drilling, blasting,
  Battling tides around the clock,
Through the depths of icy water,
  Driving caissons down to rock.

Fleets of freighters bring their cargoes
  From the forges and the kilns;
Stone and steel – ten thousand barge loads-
  From the quarries, mines and mills.

Now the towers, mounting skyward,
  Reach the heights of airy space.
Hear the rivet-hammers ringing,
  Joining steel in strength and grace.

High above the swirling currents,
  Parabolic strands are strung;
From the cables, packed with power
  Wonder-spans of steel are hung.

Generations dreamed the crossing;
  Doubters shook their heads in scorn.
Brave men vowed that they would build it-
  From their faith a bridge was born.

There it spans the miles of water,
  Speeding millions on their way;
Bridge of vision, hope and courage,
  Portal of a brighter day.

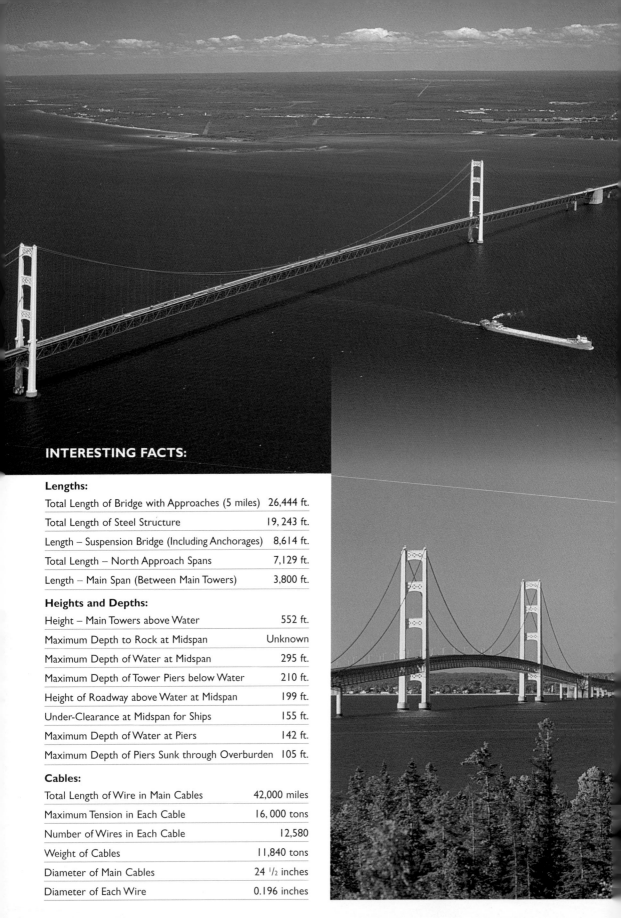

INTERESTING FACTS:

Lengths:

Total Length of Bridge with Approaches (5 miles)	26,444 ft.
Total Length of Steel Structure	19,243 ft.
Length – Suspension Bridge (Including Anchorages)	8,614 ft.
Total Length – North Approach Spans	7,129 ft.
Length – Main Span (Between Main Towers)	3,800 ft.

Heights and Depths:

Height – Main Towers above Water	552 ft.
Maximum Depth to Rock at Midspan	Unknown
Maximum Depth of Water at Midspan	295 ft.
Maximum Depth of Tower Piers below Water	210 ft.
Height of Roadway above Water at Midspan	199 ft.
Under-Clearance at Midspan for Ships	155 ft.
Maximum Depth of Water at Piers	142 ft.
Maximum Depth of Piers Sunk through Overburden	105 ft.

Cables:

Total Length of Wire in Main Cables	42,000 miles
Maximum Tension in Each Cable	16,000 tons
Number of Wires in Each Cable	12,580
Weight of Cables	11,840 tons
Diameter of Main Cables	24 1/2 inches
Diameter of Each Wire	0.196 inches

One of Michigan's greatest events, Mackinac Bridge Walk, is held each year on Labor Day at the Mackinac Bridge. The total miles walked by participants would circle the earth, at the equator, several times. In addition to the general walk, special athletic walking races are held. A really pleasant, gala day's outing, this traditional event draws between 50,000 and 70,000 participants each year.

Connecting Michigan's two great peninsulas, the graceful Mackinac Bridge has become one of the most familiar attractions in the Midwest. Each year there is an increase in traffic crossing the bridge – both commercial and pleasure.

Operated and maintained by the State of Michigan Mackinac Bridge Authority, the bridge is constantly kept in mint condition by paint and service crews.

The World's longest
suspension bridge

Tormented sky, shafts of lightning and Majestic Bridge in electrical storm

*M*ackinac Island is served by outstanding ferry boat services, both from St. Ignace and Mackinaw City. The colorful boats offer great viewing and photo opportunities of the island and its harbor as well as the mighty Mackinac Bridge and Round Island Lighthouse.

Ferry Boats

*R*ound Island Lighthouse, constructed in 1895, was in continuous use for 52 years until it was replaced by an automated beacon at the south end of Mackinac Island in 1947. This restored lighthouse is supervised by the United States Forest Service.

The lighthouse serves as a sentinel of the past, reminding visitors of the often precarious sailing and rich history of the Straits of Mackinac.

A mile away on Mackinac Island, the stately Grand Hotel can be seen.

Mackinac (pronounced Mack-in-aw) Island is three miles long, two miles wide and nine miles around at the shore. Its unique atmosphere may be attributed in part to the total lack of motorized vehicles. Transportation is by way of walking, bicycle, horseback or surrey. The century old architecture reflects a busy past when the island was the fur trading capital of this part of the continent. After the fur industry decline, rich businessmen came to the island and built summer homes. Today hundreds of thousands of visitors come to the island each summer to relax and enjoy its unusual character.

Main Street

Mackinac Island

Mackinac Island carriage tours take guests to visit many of the Island highlights and historic sites. Drivers are most informative and willing to answer questions about the region. Surrey Hill is one of the stops of the carriage tours.

The famous three horse hitch takes visitors on a fascinating tour of Historic Mackinac Island landmarks, including Arch Rock and Fort Mackinac.

photo by George M. Houghton

Beaumont Memorial, a reconstruction of the Old American Fur Company store where, in 1822, Alexis St. Martin was accidentally shot in the stomach. Dr. Beaumont, the fort surgeon, treated the wound which never completely closed. In the years that followed, Dr. Beaumont was able to discover the secret of the human digestive process by observing St. Martin's stomach through the opening.

*T*he beautiful "Butterfly House" is a tropical garden where hundreds of butterflies from around
the world dance to the sound of falling water and
classical music.

*A*rch Rock is a natural
limestone formation
with a span of 50 feet,
which rises 149 feet above
the clear blue water of the
Straits of Mackinac. It is a
highlight of the carriage
tours and is one of the
most photographed spots
on the Island.
In Indian legend, it was the
gateway to Gitchie
Manitow, great and good
spirit, Chief of all Indians.
His dwelling was a huge
wigwam which through the
years has turned to stone
and is now called Sugar
Loaf Rock.

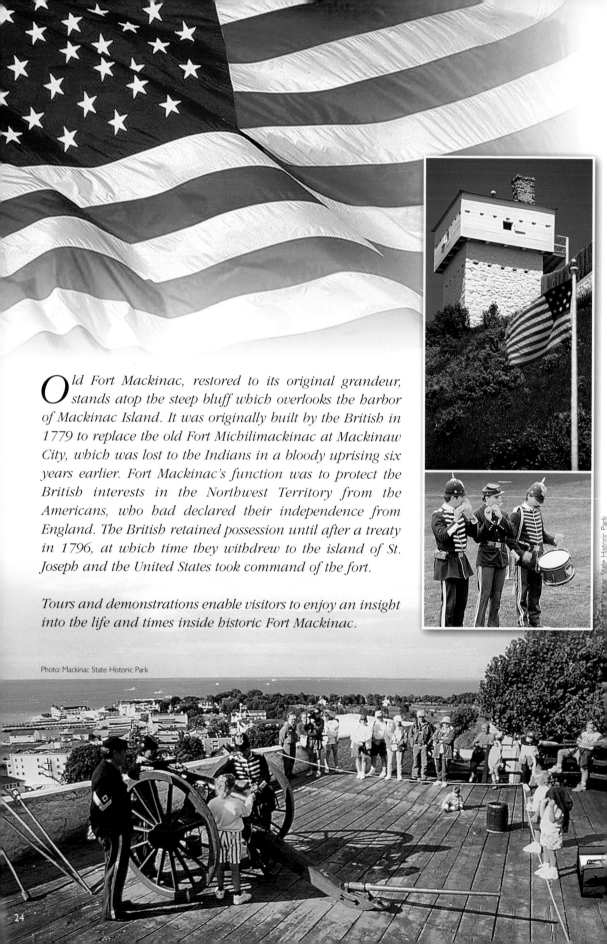

*O*ld Fort Mackinac, restored to its original grandeur, stands atop the steep bluff which overlooks the harbor of Mackinac Island. It was originally built by the British in 1779 to replace the old Fort Michilimackinac at Mackinaw City, which was lost to the Indians in a bloody uprising six years earlier. Fort Mackinac's function was to protect the British interests in the Northwest Territory from the Americans, who had declared their independence from England. The British retained possession until after a treaty in 1796, at which time they withdrew to the island of St. Joseph and the United States took command of the fort.

Tours and demonstrations enable visitors to enjoy an insight into the life and times inside historic Fort Mackinac.

Photo: Mackinac State Historic Park

Fort Mackinac

Photo: Mackinac State Historic Park

*I*n the War of 1812 between the United States and Great Britain, the fort was re-captured by the British, who dragged a cannon to a position now known as Fort Holmes, a high point behind Fort Mackinac. With this cannon in position, surrender came easily, without a battle. The American forces made several unsuccessful attempts to regain the fort during the War of 1812. At the war's end, American troops did return and took possession in 1815.

During the year of 1894, the United States garrisons left the fort and it became a part of Michigan's State Park system in 1895.

Photo: Mackinac State Historic Park

Lilac Festival

*T*he Lilac Festival is held in June when the Island's lilac trees burst forth in a spectacular
display with sweet fragrance that drifts across the entire island. Some trees are 300 years
old, brought here by the early settlers. It is a festive event complete with a parade with horse-
drawn floats and carriages.

Sailing Events

*M*ackinac Island has always lured sailors to its harbor. Each July two major sailing contests are held, one from Chicago and one from Port Huron, with Mackinac Island as their destination. There is a lot of camaraderie and rivalry, as several hundred tall masted sailing ships fill the harbor.

Little Stone Church

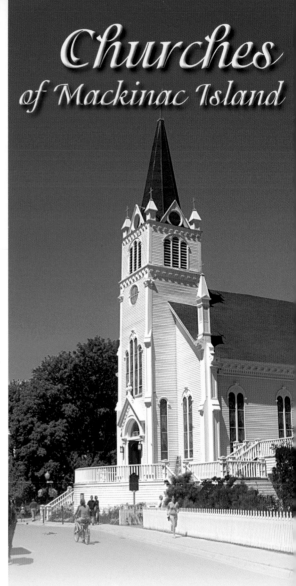

▲ Ste. Anne's Catholic Church

*F*or three centuries modern religion has played an important role in the Mackinac area. From Missionary Priests, who along with voyageurs first pioneered this territory, to our modern times, the need for spiritual leadership is still felt.

◄ Trinity Episcopal Church

Grand Hotel

*O*pened on July 10th, 1887, the Grand Hotel was built by the Grand Rapids, Indiana and Michigan Central Railroads and the Detroit and Cleveland Navigation Company.

Built of Michigan white pine it features a magnificent colonial porch (longest in the world) overlooking the Straits of Mackinac. It is an example of gracious living seldom seen today.

Grand Hotel
World's Largest
Summer Hotel